Mellie learns about the World Equestrian Games

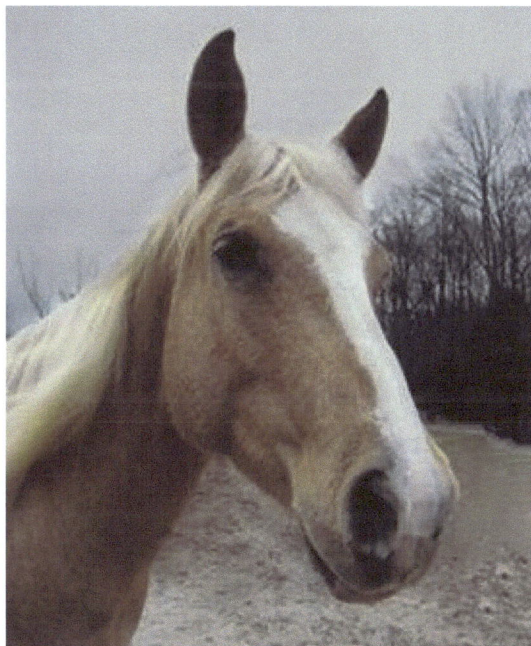

Written by Wendy Cantrell

Told by Miss Mountin Melody

The Cantrell Farm series

This book is dedicated to all the wonderful horses that touch our lives.

Their stories we hope will give a greater understanding to the many personalities and traits that make each one an individual just like us. That like us they too can be happy, sad, confident, and fearful or any of the feeling and emotions that humans have. After years of instructing others how to ride and care for horses, they never cease to amaze me.

This publication would not be possible without the help from so many. Beth Cole Grant cover, Joanne Doane illustrator, photos from Denver Cantrell, Daniel Gibbs, Aly Keay, Elizabeth Morsani, Price Story, TJ Vore, and Caroline Williamson, and the many who helped me learn how to use word.

Available from Amazon, Kindle and other retailers

IBSN-13: 987-1-7325057-0-4

Table of Contents

Mellie learns about the World Equestrian Games

Hi, my name is Miss Mountin Melody, but everyone calls me Mellie. I am an American Paint. My color is palomino.

I keep hearing about something called the World Equestrian Games. I love to play games.

There is catch my person for a treat game. Another game is go after the Frisbee.

My favorite game is to push the ball. But they do not have that in these games.

These games are held every four years somewhere in the world, with horses and riders from many countries. It is considered a major international championship.

There are different games to play: endurance, show jumping, eventing, combined driving, vaulting, reining, dressage and para-equestrian. I think if they knew how much fun the ball was to play with it could be added to these games.

One of the games is called show jumping. Actually I can show you how to jump up in the air and kick out my heels too. But they play it differently.

The horse with a rider has a course or pattern of brightly painted obstacles called jumps that the riders are allowed to walk the course, but not the horses. Some jumps are high, some wide and some close together called combinations. So when the horse is asked to jump the course, it must listen very carefully to the rider so it will know where to go.

This is Caroline on Archangel jumping parallel poles.
The jump is as wide as it is high.

If the horse knocks down any poles or refuses, they get points off. The horse and rider with the lowest points wins unless there is a tie. Then there is a jump off. The fastest time with the lowest points wins.

If the rider falls off they are eliminated. Oh, and if a horse thinks he can't jump it (the jumps are quite high and some very wide) they get two more tries. But after that they eliminated also.

Caroline on Domingo jumping a vertical.

Another game is dressage. Now I am really beautiful when I dress up.

Well, it turns out that it is more of a dance with a rider, but it is called a test. The horse has several kinds of walks, trots and canters to perform in a pattern. The movements have names, like half pass for going sideways and forward at the same time, which is really neat.

This is Elizabeth on Asian.

What looks hard is when they do piaffe. Think of trotting in place. Then there is passage where the horse looks like it is floating. Tempi changes looks like skipping. I have tried that, it is hard.

Kristina Harrison Naness riding
Rociero XV

These are turning into very hard games, but I think I could maybe do the next one. It is called para equestrian.

See my beautiful trot.

This game is for athletics with physical disabilities or vision impairment. Due to the limitations of the riders, the horse and rider team perform a dressage test at their competitive level.

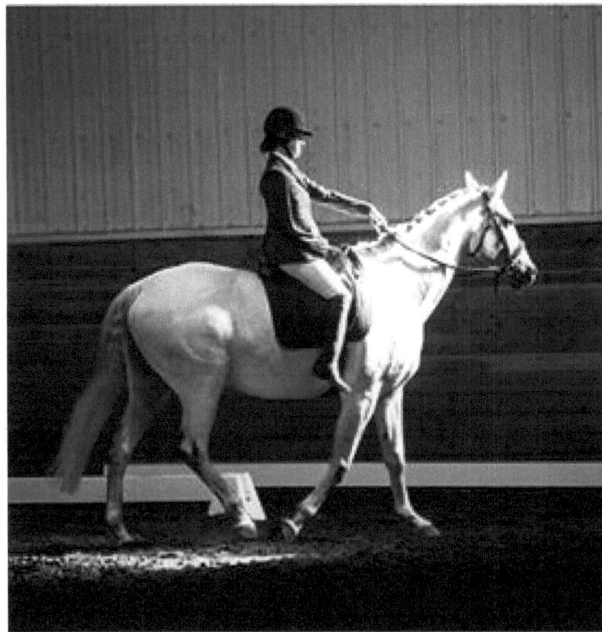

It would be an honor to try.   This is Aly Keay, para rider, saluting the judge.

Have you ever been in a really long race? I have asthma, so I can't. But I love long walks. This is me, Mellie with my friend, Maxie on a trail ride.

The WEG endurance race is a 100 mile race through the surrounding country side over a marked trail.

Veterinarians make sure the horses are in excellent physical health to compete during the race and after. The horse and rider have mandatory rest stops to get checked.

This is Shadowfax with TJ competing in a 75 mile ride race.

The first horse to cross the finish line fit to continue wins.

I noticed that most of the horses competing in this game are Arabians, known for their endurance.

We are exploring the meadow.

I look fabulous in my western saddle. I would wear it if I did reining.

When I first heard of this game I thought I had to ride in the rain. But no umbrella here.

This game has patterns to complete with precise precision. The horses must lope (a really slow canter) and gallop a circle, swapping leads when they change direction. Bet you don't know what swapping leads is? When you skip, you have a leg that stays forward. That is your leading leg. If you change direction you hop to change the leg that is leading to the other leg. That hop is a swap.

In reining the horse must also stop and spin. I don't know how they don't get dizzy. Run downs are where they gallop in a straight line sliding to a stop. The horses have special shoes on the hind feet to help them slide to a stop.

Daniel on Lotsa Big Dreams, whose barn name is Maggie

Rollbacks are also judged. This is where the horse quickly turns and runs the opposite direction after a stop. Doesn't this game sound like fun?

Daniel on Spooks Full Throttle

I am glad the game of vaulting is not a lot of jumping. But as it turns out, the rider is the one that vaults.

To do this game I have to canter round and round a person holding a long rope called a longe line. I have to show good manners and even rhythm. But I am not really large enough to do this.

The riders, some individual, some in pairs and even teams of riders perform all kinds of gymnastics on the horses back while cantering to music! There are compulsory classes and free style classes.

This is an example of a free style movement. Notice the special saddles the horses have. The riders wear clothing that will not catch on the saddle and special shoes.

The girl on the black horse is doing a compulsory move. Compulsory means required.

Now my friend, Sugar, has told me about the next game called carriage driving. Here Sugar is learning to pull a cart.

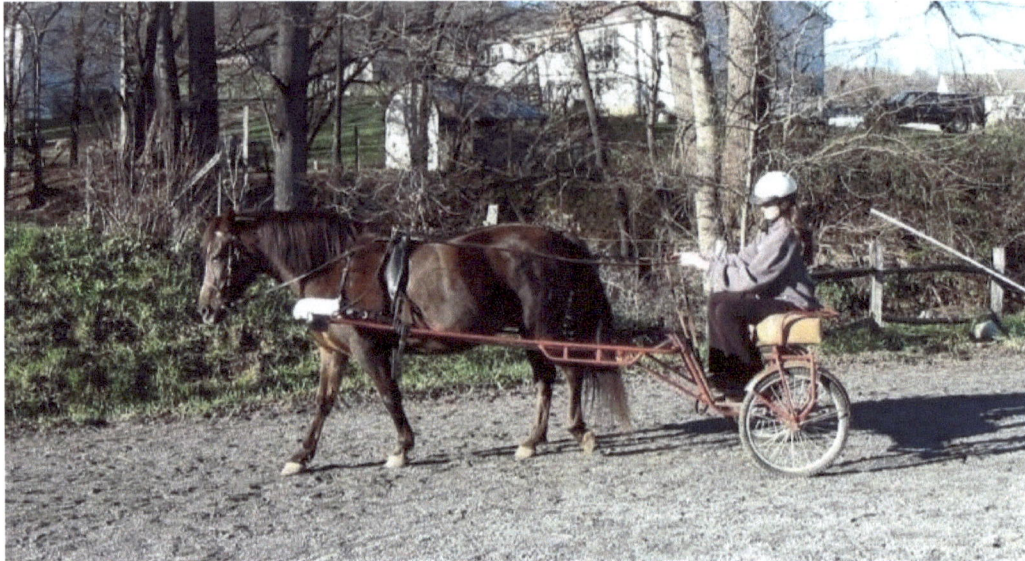

This sounds so hard but very exciting. A single horse, two horses or a team of four horses can compete in their division. Each division has three types of tests to do. There is a winner in each division that has the highest combined test score.

The first test is a dressage test which also includes a presentation. Horses, drivers, groom and equipment must meet certain standards of safety and cleanliness.

The second is a marathon test. In a marathon the teams negotiate obstacles out in the field, sometimes going through water or up and down steep hills. It is not for speed. There is a maximum and minimum time in which to complete the course.

The third is obstacle cone course driving. With all those cones in the ring, I don't see how they remember where to go. You look closely you will see balls on the cones. They get penalties if those are knocked down or if they go too slow.

Linda Willis with her pair of adorable ponies.

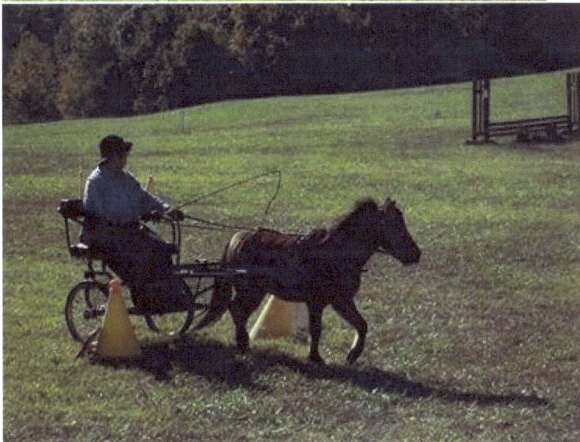

Eve Arnsberg and her pony Oliver.

.

Price and her Swedish Gotland pony, Kokovoko Halley. This is a very rare breed.

The last game is called eventing. I was ready to get dressed up and go eat. Isn't that what you do when you go to an event?

My friend, Joy told me that was not what it is as she has competed in many with her person, Denver.

This game has three parts like carriage driving with dressage being first. The judge wants to see a horse cooperate with balance, rhythm and suppleness.

Elizabeth on Sonrisa TLM

The second part is called cross country. It consists of riding a course across the country side with thirty to forty jumps.

 There is a minimum and maximum time frame like carriage driving. There are penalties and possible elimination for refusing a fence. They can get eliminated for other mistakes as well.

There are all kinds of jumps like this bank and the big log Joy and Denver are jumping.

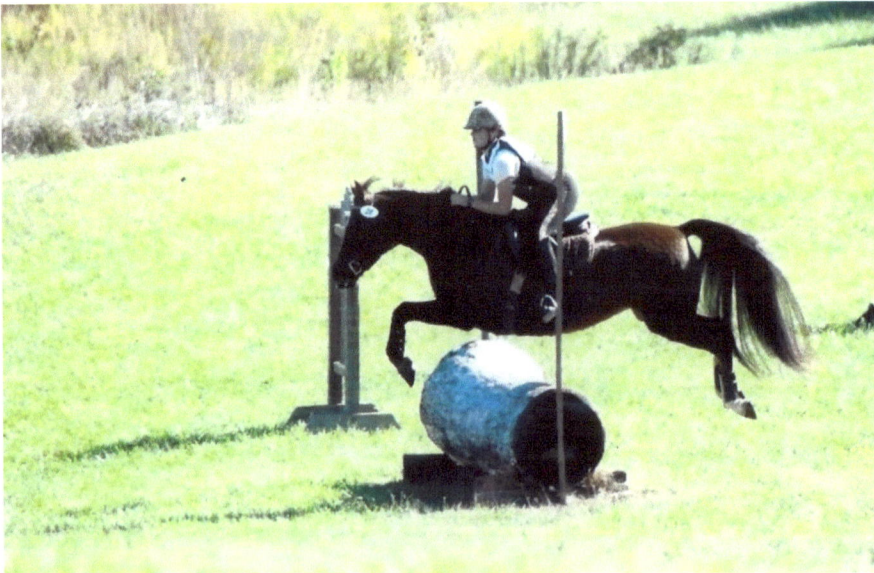

The third part is show jumping where the horse/rider team need strong technical skills. (Technical skills means they really know what they are doing.)

The jumps are easily knocked down. There also is a time limit to complete the course. In a jump off the fastest time with least penalties wins.

Some of the jumps are high and some wide with combinations of jumps close together. If the horse or rider falls, it is elimination, same if the horse refuses the jump twice. All these courses are twisty and long. Going the wrong way will get them eliminated also.

These are some pictures of Denver and Joy learning the skills at a lower level.

Next time I get invited to play games, I am definitely asking what kind.

Sugar, Maxie, Joy and others have many stories to tell. Look for their books. In the meantime, I think I will take a nap.

Notes